Rationalizations
To Live By

Rationalizations
To Live By

By Henry Beard • Andy Borowitz
and John Boswell

Illustrated by Roz Chast

WORKMAN PUBLISHING • NEW YORK

Library of Congress Cataloging-in-Publication Data

Rationalizations to live by /
Henry Beard (et al.).

p.cm.

ISBN 0-7611-1636-2

1. Excuses—Humor.
2. Rationalization (Psychology—Humor. I. Beard, Henry.

PN6231.E87 M56 2000
818'.5402—dc21   00-020108

Workman books are available at special discounts when purchased
in bulk for premiums and sales promotions as well as for fund-raising
or educational use. Special editions or book excerpts can also be
created to specifications. For details, contact the Special Sales Director
at the address below.

WORKMAN PUBLISHING
708 Broadway
New York, NY 10003

www.workman.com

Manufactured in the United States of America

First printing April 2000

10 9 8 7 6 5 4 3 2 1

An "excuse" is a lie
we tell others.

•

A "rationalization"
is a lie we tell ourselves.

When I get back from this trip,
I'm going on a diet.

My parents don't want me
coming home any more than
I want to be there.

I'm this way because
of my parents.

•

My parents are this way
because of their parents.

•

My kids are this way
because of my parents.

Hot tubs are great
for resale.

•

I only bought the cell phone
for the car.

•

Wide-screen TVs are easier
on your eyes.

I'll save even more money
if I buy nine of these.

If I do a really good job,
nobody'll care that it's twelve
weeks late.

Greed is good.

The red wine is doing wonders
for my cholesterol.

•

If we don't finish this second
bottle, it'll just go bad.

•

We're all going to die
of something.

Look how long the French live.

I need this nose job for my
breathing passages.

•

Bigger breasts will be good
for my career.

•

While I'm getting my appendix
out, I might as well have
my face lifted.

I was blond as a child.

She's probably
cheating on me, too.

Dating twenty-year-olds
is good for my self-esteem.

•

This doesn't really count
as sex.

•

I'm not running for "saint."

This is "tough love."

Lobsters don't feel pain.

I do some of my best thinking
on the golf course.

•

I'm fertilizing these bushes.

I'm only moving the ball to where it should have landed.

If I were in the hospital,
I wouldn't want a bunch of
people bothering me.

If I stop at this accident,
I'll just get in the way.

No one will ever know.

My vote doesn't make a difference.

I've never
been good with authority.

If he leaves it out on his desk,
it's OK to read it.

I never smoke in the house.

•

I only smoke at parties.

•

I could quit tomorrow.

•

After going all day
without smoking, I deserve
a cigarette.

This is my last one.

I didn't know him that well.

All this shopping
is good for the economy.

After a crummy day
like this, I deserve
these shoes.

•

After a great day
like this, I should celebrate
with these shoes.

•

With what I saved on
this purse, I should buy
these shoes.

He'll just spend it on liquor.

•

If he's really crippled, how'd he make it to the corner?

•

If he's so poor, where'd he get the pen to make that cardboard sign?

I'll do a better job on this
if I start first thing
in the morning.

•

These dishes will be easier
to clean if I let them
soak overnight.

•

My clothes won't get so
wrinkled if I pack tomorrow.

I can't help it, it's genetic.

I'm just big-boned.

•

European sizes are smaller.

•

Skipping one day
of exercise isn't going
to kill me.

I'm not as fat as those people in the mall.

Like I'm the only one who's
peed in this pool?

That's for the one you called
"out" last game.

•

That's for trying to drill
me with the overhead.

•

That's for being such
an asshole.

At least I didn't sell out.

Dear Mr. Higsbee:

I just wanted to tell you what a great job I think you're doing here at Axelrod Hatbands. Your intelligence, wit, courage, and dynamic leadership are — or indeed, SHOULD be — inspiration to us all. I am constantly amazed at how you manage to learn new →

It's not sucking up to the boss if you really mean it.

Everybody does it.

I'm not trying to win a popularity contest.

$4,000

This designer dress is really an investment.

What are the odds of a
handicapped person needing
this spot while I drop off
my video?

I have a lot of anger.

I'm not doing as bad a job as my parents did.

My kid's grades are bad
because he's bored.

My kid's too creative
for this school.

My kid will get a lot out
of military school.

If God didn't want us to eat baby sheep, he wouldn't have given us mint jelly.

•

If God didn't want us to eat beef, he wouldn't have given us steak sauce.

God doesn't give a shit
what we eat.

It's deductible.

The mink was already dead.

It's for a good cause.

This'll be a good
experience for the kids.

•

I spend quality time
with my kids.

•

Children need time
to be alone.

If I had studied harder,
my answers would have been
less spontaneous.

If I practice more
it will sound...rehearsed.

I'm only human.

They pay ushers to clean
this stuff up.

He'll be happy with Poland.

Anyone dumb enough to fall
for that big wooden horse
deserves to lose.

•

We had to destroy the village
in order to save it.

I'm not going to screw up my kids by leaving them money.

Video games are good for my
kid's motor skills.

My work was never intended
for the masses.

I.Q. tests don't measure creativity.

•

I have *emotional* intelligence.

•

I just don't test well.

I'm earning frequent-flier miles.

•

You make great contacts
in First Class.

It's not littering if it's
biodegradable.

Einstein had a messy desk.

I love her for her mind,
not her huge tits.

He'll thank me later.

My wife doesn't understand me.

I'm a very sexual person.

If snails didn't want to be eaten,
they'd speed up.

I'll wait for the
paperback.

•

I'll wait for the movie.

•

I'll wait for the video.

It's not like he's never borrowed
something from me
and not returned it.

•

Finders keepers.

Ice cream is an excellent source
of calcium.

I'll be dead by then.

Picasso didn't do his
best work until he was seventy.

Everybody lies about sex.

These lesbian
lovemaking scenes are very
artistically done.

Everybody cheats on their taxes.

It's the thought that counts.

Nobody died.

DELUXE SUITE	$2340.
ROOM SERVICE	675.
RESTAURANTS	922.
MASSAGES	125.
BATHROBE	100.
LIMOUSINES	480.
MANICURE	50.

This expense sheet makes up
for my crappy bonus.

He's good with the children.

I'm eating for two now.

You can't concentrate on
a serious book at the beach.

It's not plagiarism, it's an "homage."

I don't photograph well.

You only live once.

People like short books
with big type.